HEROES OF BLACK HISTORY

HARRIET TUBMAN

BY JANEY LEVY

Gareth Stevens
PUBLISHING

Please visit our website, www.garethstevens.com. For a free color catalog of all our high-quality books, call toll free 1-800-542-2595 or fax 1-877-542-2596.

Library of Congress Cataloging-in-Publication Data
Names: Levy, Janey, author.
Title: Harriet Tubman / Janey Levy.
Description: New York : Gareth Stevens Publishing, [2021] | Series: Heroes of Black History | Includes index.
Identifiers: LCCN 2019046809 | ISBN 9781538258163 (library binding) | ISBN 9781538258149 (paperback) | ISBN 9781538258156 (6 Pack) | ISBN 9781538258170 (ebook)
Subjects: LCSH: Tubman, Harriet, 1822-1913–Juvenile literature. | Slaves–United States–Biography–Juvenile literature. | African American women–Biography–Juvenile literature. | African Americans–Biography–Juvenile literature. | Underground Railroad–Juvenile literature.
Classification: LCC E444.T82 L49 2021 | DDC 326/.8092 [B]–dc23
LC record available at https://lccn.loc.gov/2019046809

First Edition

Published in 2021 by
Gareth Stevens Publishing
111 East 14th Street, Suite 349
New York, NY 10003

Designer: Laura Bowen
Editor: Monika Davies

Photo credits: Cover, pp. 1 (Harriet Tubman and background), 5, 21, 27 courtesy of the Library of Congress; p. 7 Universal Images Group/Universal Images Group Editorial/Getty Images; p. 9 Mondadori Portfolio/Contributor/Getty Images; p. 11 Eliza Ann Brodess/Wikimedia Commons; p. 13 (map) Weredragon/Shutterstock.com; p. 13 (inset) Sharon Cole/Shutterstock.com; p. 15 The Washington Post/Contributor; p. 17 Universal History Archive/Contributor/Universal Images Group/Getty Images; p. 19 PhillipJR/Shutterstock.com; p. 21 (inset) Tikky19/Wikimedia Commons; p. 23 Education Images/Contributor/Universal Images Group Editorial/Getty Images; p. 25 (main) PhotoQuest/Contributor/Archive Photos/Getty Images; p. 25 (inset) Napoleon Sarony/Wikimedia Commons; p. 26 Lvklock/Wikimedia Commons.

Printed in the United States of America

CPSIA compliance information: Batch #CS20GS: For further information contact Gareth Stevens, New York, New York at 1-800-542-2595.

CONTENTS

Words in the glossary appear in **bold** type the first time they are used in the text.

SAY HELLO TO HARRIET

Harriet Tubman is remembered in history as a brave and bold hero. She was born into slavery in the early 1800s, enduring much suffering at a young age. She later managed to escape to freedom in the northern United States. Then, despite considerable danger, she returned to the South multiple times to aid other slaves and help them escape slavery.

When the **American Civil War** began, she worked as both a spy and leader for the North. This often meant placing herself in great danger again. After the war, she continued to help freed slaves and also **advocated** for women's rights. You'll learn more about this remarkable woman inside this book.

SLAVERY IN THE UNITED STATES

In 1619, the first Africans were captured and taken to the British colonies in North America. The first slave law in the colonies was passed in 1641. During Harriet's life, the number of slaves in the United States rose from about 1.5 million to nearly 4 million by the time the American Civil War started.

Harriet Tubman was a small woman, only about 5 feet (1.5 m) tall.

BORN INTO SLAVERY

Harriet Tubman was born into slavery around 1820 in Dorchester County, Maryland. Her parents, Harriet Green and Benjamin Ross, originally named her Araminta Ross.

Harriet was nicknamed Minty as a young child. As she was born into slavery, Minty didn't have much of a childhood. Starting when she was about 5 years old, she was rented out to other **plantation** owners as a house servant. The plantation owners often beat Minty when they were unhappy with her. When she was about 12 years old, Minty went to work in the fields. It was around this time that she suffered a head **injury** that caused lifelong problems for her.

WHEN WAS TUBMAN BORN?

As Harriet was born into slavery, her exact date of birth was never recorded. Her date of birth is lost in history, though she was likely born sometime between 1820 and 1825. Harriet believed she was born in 1825. However, her death record states she was born in 1815, and her grave marker says she was born "about 1820."

This photo shows adults and children living in slavery on a large plantation in South Carolina. Tubman lived on the Brodess Farm, a smaller plantation.

Even as a child, Minty had the courage to stand up to the wrongs of slavery. When she was young, she once blocked a doorway to protect another slave from an angry overseer, or boss. The overseer threw a heavy weight that hit Minty in the head. Minty never fully recovered from her terrible injury.

For the rest of her life, Minty suffered from bad headaches. She also experienced times where she fell into a deep sleep. It was impossible to wake her during these sleeping spells. The plantation owner that Minty belonged to tried to sell her, but no one wanted to buy a slave who had sleeping spells.

BECOMING HARRIET TUBMAN

Around 1844, Minty married a free black man named John Tubman. She took his last name and changed her first name to Harriet, in honor of her mother. She now had the name she's known by today. However, although her husband was free, Harriet remained a slave.

Slaves often worked in the fields from sunrise to sunset. During the summertime, this could equal 14 hours of work.

In 1849, the plantation owner died, leaving behind a farm with a large amount of debt. The family started selling the slaves that belonged to the farm to other slave owners in order to pay off the debt. Harriet didn't want to be sold to a plantation farther South, so she made plans to escape. She ended up going by herself, leaving behind her husband, parents, sisters, and brothers.

On her journey, both black and white helpers aided Harriet, sheltering her and giving guidance to where she should go next. Harriet's escape would mark her first experience with the Underground Railroad.

THE UNDERGROUND RAILROAD

The Underground Railroad was the name for a secret network, or system, of people and places that helped runaway slaves escape to freedom in the northern United States and Canada. People who guided slaves to safety were "conductors." Safe places for slaves to stay were "stations." People who hid slaves were "station masters." Escaping slaves were "passengers."

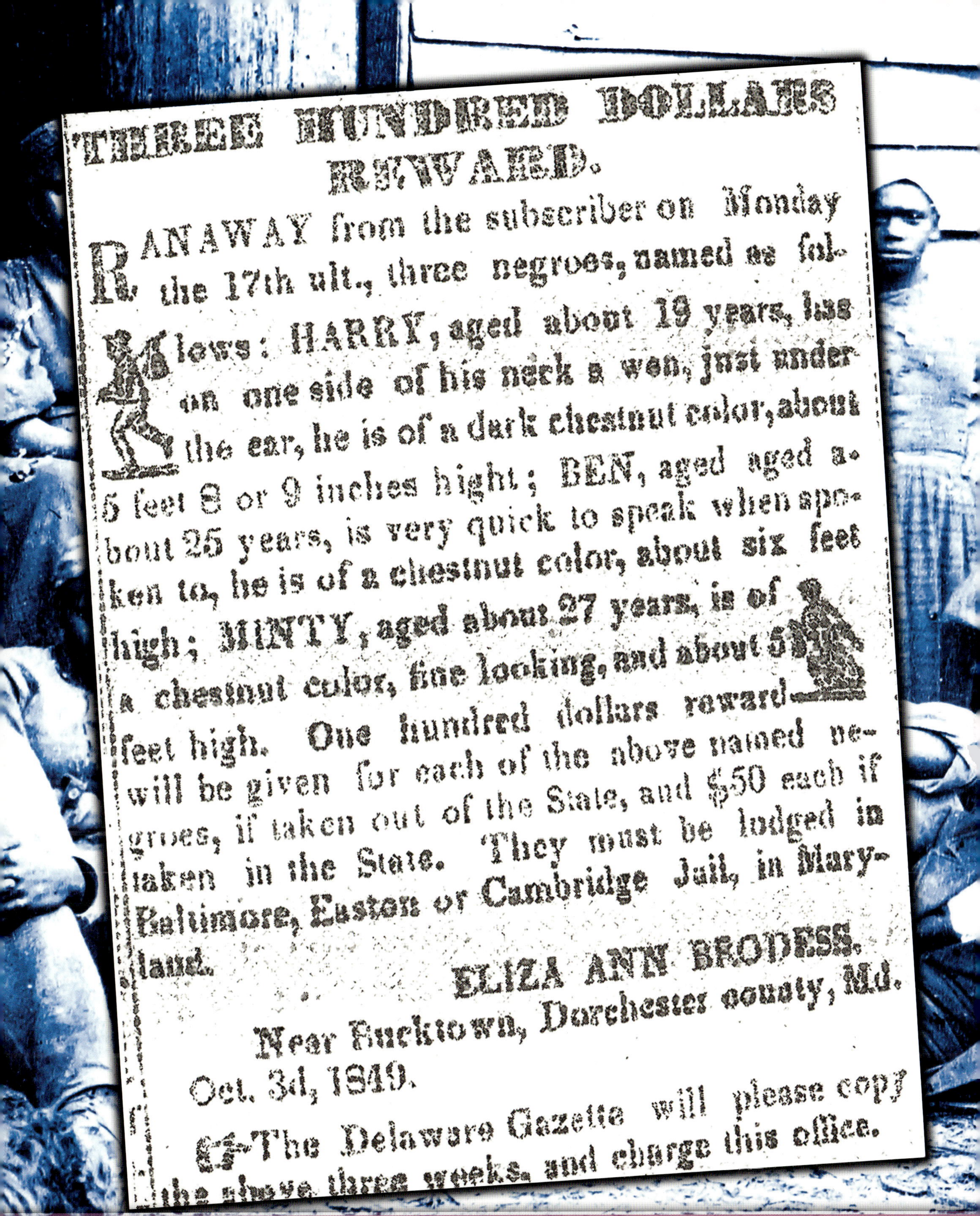

THREE HUNDRED DOLLARS REWARD.

RANAWAY from the subscriber on Monday the 17th ult., three negroes, named as follows: HARRY, aged about 19 years, has on one side of his neck a wen, just under the ear, he is of a dark chestnut color, about 5 feet 8 or 9 inches hight; BEN, aged aged about 25 years, is very quick to speak when spoken to, he is of a chestnut color, about six feet high; MINTY, aged about 27 years, is of a chestnut color, fine looking, and about 5 feet high. One hundred dollars reward will be given for each of the above named negroes, if taken out of the State, and $50 each if taken in the State. They must be lodged in Baltimore, Easton or Cambridge Jail, in Maryland.

ELIZA ANN BRODESS.

Near Bucktown, Dorchester county, Md.

Oct. 3d, 1849.

☞The Delaware Gazette will please copy the above three weeks, and charge this office.

Harriet escaped twice. A reward notice was posted for her return after the first try. Her brothers are also named, as they first set out to escape with her. But they became frightened and turned back. Later, Harriet escaped again—alone.

FINDING NORTH

Harriet made part of her journey to freedom on foot. She traveled at night to avoid being spotted by slave catchers. Harriet knew she wanted to go north, so she followed the North Star in the night sky to find her way.

No one knows exactly what route Harriet followed. Some believe she may have followed the Choptank River and traveled through Delaware before reaching Pennsylvania. She settled in Philadelphia, Pennsylvania, where slavery was outlawed and she was able to support herself doing different jobs. She was a free woman, but her family was still living in slavery. Harriet planned to rescue them.

THE NORTH STAR

Slaves used the constellation, or group of stars, called the Big Dipper to find the North Star. Two stars on the dipper's edge point to the North Star. They also looked for moss on trees to find their way north. This is because moss usually grows on the north side of trees.

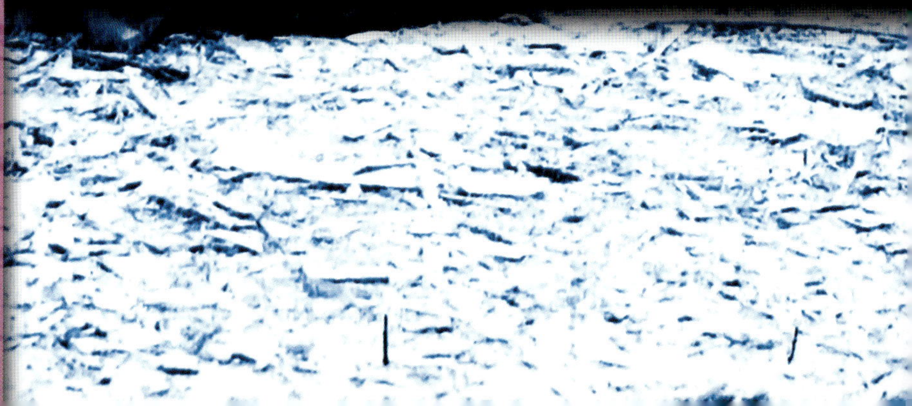

ROUTE TO FREEDOM?

This map shows the possible route Harriet followed to escape slavery from Dorchester County, Maryland, to Philadelphia, Pennsylvania. She might have traveled alongside the Choptank River to escape.

UNDERGROUND RAILROAD CONDUCTOR

Harriet was driven to help other slaves reach freedom, starting with her own family. It wasn't long before the onetime passenger on the Underground Railroad became a conductor. In late 1850, she made her first trip back to Maryland to rescue her niece, as well as her niece's two children, in order to lead them to freedom.

As a runaway slave, it was dangerous for Harriet to return to Maryland. She might have been caught and returned to the plantation she escaped from. But Harriet was fearless. Soon after her first journey, she returned to rescue more members of her family.

THE FUGITIVE SLAVE ACT OF 1850

To help slave owners, the U.S. Congress passed the Fugitive Slave Act of 1850. It stated people could capture and return runaway slaves to their original owners. This included runaway slaves who'd escaped to free states, or places that didn't have slavery. The act also made it illegal for anyone to help escaped slaves.

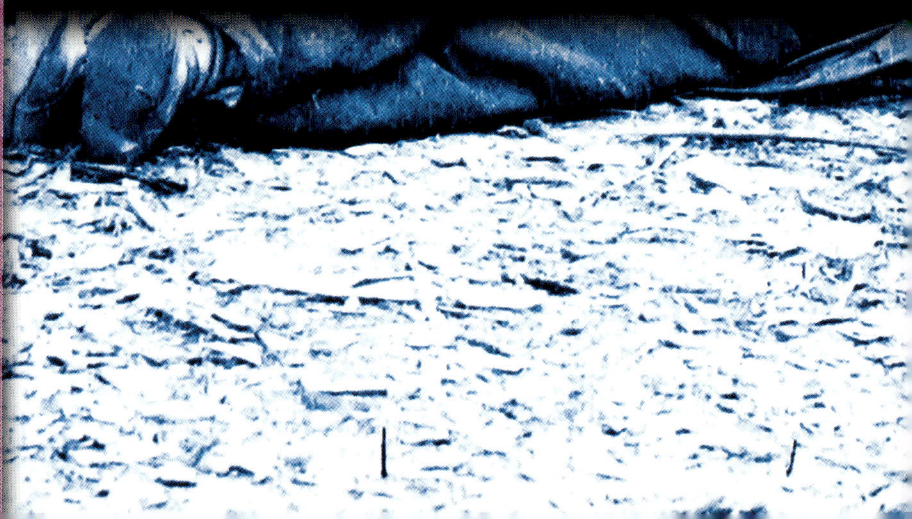

This building on a Maryland farm was a station on the Underground Railroad.

On another trip back to Maryland, Harriet contacted her husband. She hoped he would follow her north and join her in Philadelphia. But since she had left him behind in Maryland, he'd married someone else and wanted to stay in Maryland. Because he was already a free man, he didn't need to journey to Philadelphia for freedom.

Harriet continued to return to Maryland to rescue slaves for the next 10 years. Her parents were some of the last people she rescued. The journey north was hard because her **elderly** parents were unable to walk many miles. But she managed to get them safely to the north.

THE MOSES OF HER PEOPLE

William Lloyd Garrison, a well-known **abolitionist**, called Harriet "Moses" for her courage in leading slaves to freedom. He was comparing her to Moses in the Bible, who led Jews out of slavery in Egypt. As a conductor on the Underground Railroad, Harriet once said she "never ran [her] train off the track and never lost a passenger."

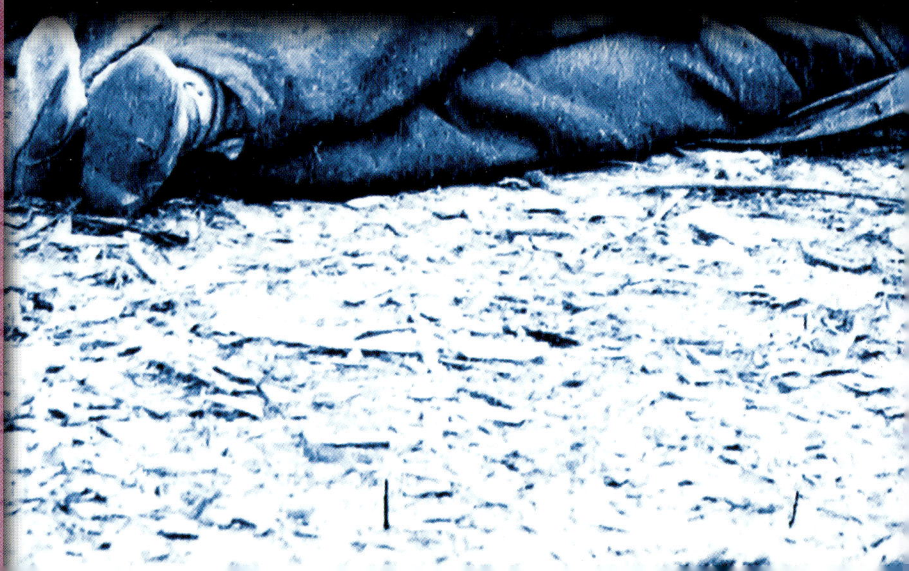

This illustration shows slaves traveling along the Underground Railroad on a dark, rainy night. It gives a sense of how hard and miserable the journey could be.

How many rescue trips did Harriet make, and how many slaves did she rescue? It's impossible to know for certain. Since many stories have turned Harriet into a larger-than-life hero, the details in these stories can't always be trusted. Recent studies show she probably made between 11 and 13 trips. She likely rescued about 70 slaves, although others found their way north by themselves using instructions from her.

Tales also say a $40,000 reward was offered for Harriet's capture. That's only a myth though. But whatever the truth may be, Harriet was a courageous leader. Few people at the time dared to do what she did.

TRICKS OF THE TRADE

Harriet used several methods to make sure her rescue trips succeeded. She sometimes took the plantation owner's horse and wagon for the first part of the escape. She wore disguises and also sang particular songs to let other people know if a situation was safe or unsafe.

This statue in Boston, Massachusetts, is a tribute to Harriet for all of her bravery during her years as a conductor for the Underground Railroad. A tribute is something that shows respect for someone.

CIVIL WAR SPY

Perhaps Tubman would have gone on rescuing slaves, but national events changed the course of her life. In 1861, the American Civil War erupted. This was a U.S. war fought between Northern states (the Union) and Southern states (the Confederacy). Harriet offered her services to the Union army.

In early 1862, Tubman headed to South Carolina to assist Union forces under the command of Colonel James Montgomery. She provided nursing care to black soldiers and newly freed slaves who filled the camps. She also was spying behind Confederate lines, showing all the courage she had shown in rescuing slaves.

HARRIET TUBMAN, NURSE

Tubman had no formal training as a nurse. Having grown up as a slave, she had never received any education. She had, however, learned how to use plants to treat illness and infection, or sickness caused by germs. She used this knowledge effectively during the American Civil War.

COLONEL JAMES MONTGOMERY

This illustration shows a Union army raid, or a sudden attack, on a rice plantation near the Combahee River in South Carolina. Harriet was part of a similar raid.

On her spying missions, Harriet discovered the locations of Confederate supplies and **ammunition**. She reported this to Montgomery, who could then carefully plan attacks. Harriet accompanied Montgomery on a big attack in June 1863.

The big attack hit several plantations along the Combahee River. It destroyed supplies of cotton, food, and weapons. The attack was also pivotal, or important, as the Union army rescued more than 700 slaves. Many of the freed slaves then joined the Union army. The June 1863 strike ended up being a serious blow to the Confederate economy. Newspaper articles about the attack celebrated Harriet's role in its success.

BLACK SOLDIERS IN THE CIVIL WAR

Black soldiers played an important part in the Civil War. Many of the soldiers led by Montgomery were freed slaves. By the time the war ended, about 179,000 black men had served in the Union army. Around 19,000 black men were in the Union navy. During the war, almost 40,000 black soldiers died, most of sickness or infection.

The Union army began **recruiting** black soldiers in 1862.

SUFFRAGIST AND HUMANITARIAN

Harriet didn't want to stop her **activism** after the Civil War ended. She saw too many causes that still needed championing in the world. At this time in history, women were refused the right to vote. They still didn't have the same rights as men. Because of this, Harriet went to work alongside **suffragists**, including Susan B. Anthony and Elizabeth Cady Stanton.

Harriet traveled and gave speeches in support of women's suffrage, using the story of her own struggle for freedom as she argued for women's **equality**. She was an activist for black women's rights and co-founded the National Association of Colored Women. She spoke at the association's first meeting in 1896.

ABOLITIONISTS AND SUFFRAGISTS

Susan B. Anthony and Elizabeth Cady Stanton weren't only passionate about the suffragist movement. Both women were also abolitionists. During the Civil War, they created the Women's Loyal National League. It campaigned for the end of slavery and full citizenship for newly freed slaves. It also collected money to give to Harriet's work.

SUSAN B. ANTHONY

ELIZABETH CADY STANTON

The idea that women should vote was first widely proposed in 1848. Many people—even women—were shocked by the suggestion at that time.

Harriet cared for many old, poor black people in her home in Auburn, New York. However, she wanted to do more for them. Harriet hoped to create a nursing home where aged black people could still live and be cared for after her death.

In 1896, when she was 74 years old, Harriet bought the 25 acres (10 ha) that sat next door to her own land. This was where the Tubman Home for Aged and **Indigent** Negroes was built. Harriet herself became a patient there in 1911 and died there in 1913.

MAKING THE DREAM A REALITY

Harriet wasn't able to collect enough money to open and run the Tubman Home. She instead turned the property over to the African Methodist Episcopal Zion Church in return for them opening and running the nursing home. The Tubman Home was open and in use from 1908 until the early 1920s.

This shows Harriet as she looked near the end of her life. After her death, she was buried with military honors at Fort Hill Cemetery in Auburn.

HERO OF FREEDOM

Today, Harriet is celebrated as a hero of freedom. Once you've heard her story, it's easy to see why. She was born a slave and, as a slave, **denied** an education. She was **physically** small. At a young age, she also suffered a terrible injury that had lifelong effects.

Yet in spite of everything that seemed to work against her, Harriet freed herself and then went on to free many more. She put herself in danger over and over again in the cause of freedom. She labored not only in the abolitionist cause, but also in the suffragist cause. Harriet's story is remarkable—and so was she.

FINAL WORDS

Harriet died of pneumonia, or an illness that affects the lungs and makes it hard to breathe. She didn't pass away alone though, and many friends and family members were by her side when she died. It's been said by some that her final words were: "I go to prepare a place for you."

A TIMELINE OF HARRIET'S LIFE

ca.1822	Harriet is born as Araminta Ross in Dorchester County, Maryland.
ca.1826	Rented out to other plantation owners as house slave
ca.1833	Begins work as field slave and later suffers terrible head injury
ca.1844	Marries John Tubman and changes name to Harriet Tubman
1849	Escapes slavery and settles in Philadelphia
1850	Begins work as conductor on the Underground Railroad
1861	Offers services to the Union army
1862	Joins soldiers of Colonel James Montgomery in South Carolina
1863	Takes part in Combahee River attack that frees more than 700 slaves
1865	Starts giving speeches for women's rights and also begins to care for aged, poor black people
1896	Buys land for the Tubman Home for Aged and Indigent Negroes
1913	Dies in Auburn, New York

GLOSSARY

abolitionist: one who fights to end slavery

activism: the use or support of actions to advocate changes in politics or society

advocate: one who supports or speaks in favor of something

American Civil War: a war fought from 1861 to 1865 in the United States between the Union (the Northern states) and the Confederacy (the Southern states)

ammunition: bullets, shells, and other things fired by weapons

deny: to refuse to give something to someone

elderly: aged

equality: the state of being equal

indigent: very poor

injury: hurt or harm

physical: having to do with the body

plantation: a large farm

recruit: to get someone to sign up for the military

suffragist: a person who worked to get the right of voting for people who did not have it

FOR MORE INFORMATION

BOOKS

Buckley, James, Jr. *Harriet Tubman: Fighter for Freedom!* San Diego, CA: Printers Row Publishing Group, 2020.

Doak, Robin S. *Harriet Tubman.* New York, NY: Children's Press, 2016.

Petry, Ann. *Harriet Tubman: Conductor on the Underground Railroad.* New York, NY: Amistad, 2018.

WEBSITES

Explore: Harriet Tubman
www.pbs.org/black-culture/explore/harriet-tubman/
Find out more interesting facts about Harriet Tubman here.

Harriet Tubman
www.americaslibrary.gov/aa/tubman/aa_tubman_subj.html
Read a short account of Tubman's life on this site.

Harriet Tubman, Spy
kids.nationalgeographic.com/explore/history/harriet-tubman
Discover more about Tubman's work as a Union spy during the Civil War.

Publisher's note to educators and parents: Our editors have carefully reviewed these websites to ensure that they are suitable for students. Many websites change frequently, however, and we cannot guarantee that a site's future contents will continue to meet our high standards of quality and educational value. Be advised that students should be closely supervised whenever they access the Internet.

INDEX